Get Ready to Play
Tee Ball

Text and Photographs by Jan Cheripko

Boyds Mills Press

Dedication

This book is dedicated to Jim "Willie" Williamson, Bill Voegelin, Rose Stachowiak, Rich Wallace, Tina Hoehn-Figura, Eric Orr, William Albronda, Scott Leet, and thousands and thousands of other volunteer coaches who give and have given their time to help boys and girls have fun.

Text and photographs copyright © 1999 by Jan Cheripko
Aerial photograph on page 7 by Chris Stein

Published by Caroline House
Boyds Mills Press, Inc.
815 Church Street
Honesdale, Pennsylvania 18431
Printed in China

Publisher Cataloging-in-Publication Data

Cheripko, Jan.
Tee Ball Fun / by Jan Cheripko.—1st edition.
[32]p. : col. ill.; cm.
Summary: Tee Ball basics, and the rules of the game, are presented here for young children.
ISBN 1-56397-716-8
I. Ballgames– Juvenile literature 2. Baseball–Juvenile literature.
[I. Ballgames. 2. Baseball.] I. Title.
796.357–dc2I 1999 CIP
LC Card Number 98-73074

Book designed by Randy Liewellyn
The text of this book is set in 12-point Helvetica Textbook.

Foreword

People play games to have fun. And Tee Ball is a game for kids to have fun. When my daughter, Julia, wanted to play Tee Ball a few years ago, my wife, Val, and I told her that winning or losing didn't matter. What mattered was that she had fun playing.

I think that the more you understand how to play a game, the more fun you can have playing it. So to understand the game better, Julia and I would play catch, and she would practice hitting the ball to me.

I thought it would be great if there were books about how to play Tee Ball so that Julia could see how other kids caught, threw, and hit the ball, and how they ran the bases. But I didn't find too many books about Tee Ball that I thought would help. There were lots of books about baseball, showing older kids or professional baseball players. There were some long books for parents and coaches about Tee Ball and baseball. However, I didn't find too many books that showed little kids, like Julia, having fun learning how to play Tee Ball. So I decided to write **Get Ready to Play Tee Ball**.

Get Ready to Play Tee Ball includes many photographs and step-by-step descriptions for beginners and their parents. My hope is that a child, parent, or coach looking for some tips about throwing, catching, hitting, running, or knowing a few of the rules of Tee Ball might find some help by turning to a section in this book.

I wrote **Get Ready to Play Tee Ball** for kids and parents and coaches all over the country and even throughout the world to help us all remember that . . .

...the purpose of playing Tee Ball is to
have fun!

Words to Get Started

Ball:
It's small, round, and often white. You hit it, throw it, and catch it.

Base:
There are four bases—first base, second base, third base, and home base (which is also called home plate).

Bat:
It has a fat part, called the meat, and a skinny part, called the handle. You use the bat to hit the ball.

Batter:
When you use the bat to hit the ball, you are the batter.

Glove:
You wear it on your hand to help you catch the ball.

Infielders:
They stand near the bases and try to catch the ball.

Outfielders:
They stand behind the infielders and try to catch the ball when it is hit past the infielders.

Runner:
After you have hit the ball and run to first base, you become a base runner.

Tee:
The ball sits on top of the tee when you get ready to hit the ball.

Webbing:
The wide part of the glove between your thumb and index finger.

Millions of children play **Tee Ball**.

Tee Ball was created for kids who are just starting to play **baseball**. In Tee Ball the ball is placed on a tee so that it is easier to hit.

It's called a tee because it's like a tee that golfers use when they play golf, only it's much bigger.

The more you know about Tee Ball, the more fun you can have playing the game.

To play Tee Ball you need a **field**.
This is what a field looks like from an airplane.

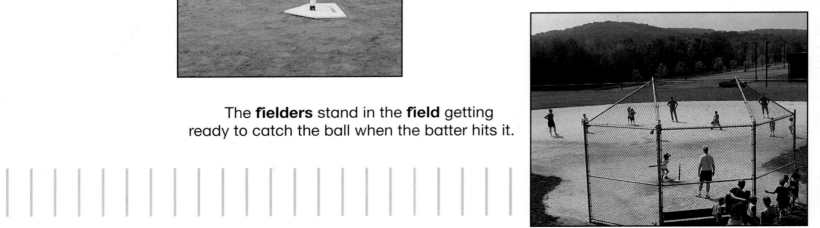

The first thing to know is that the **batter** stands at **home plate** and then hits the ball off the tee.

The **fielders** stand in the **field** getting ready to catch the ball when the batter hits it.

Let's start with hitting, because the game really begins when the batter hits the ball.

In baseball the ball is thrown fast and hard, so batters wear helmets to protect their heads while they are batting. Because the ball is not thrown in Tee Ball, some teams do not require players to wear helmets. However, if you play baseball or softball, wearing a helmet is very important, and it's a good idea to get used to wearing one.

The **batters** are the players who hold the bat and hit the ball. Sometimes they are also called the **hitters**.

The first thing you need to do to hit is to find a bat that is just right for you. If it is too heavy, you won't be able to swing it very well. If it is too light, you will swing it too quickly.

Once you have the bat you want to use, get ready to hit the ball. And here's how you do that.

If you are **right-handed**, wrap the fingers of your **left** hand around the handle of the bat toward the bottom. (The handle is the skinnier part of the bat.)

Then, wrap the fingers of your **right** hand around the handle of the bat just above your left hand. Your hands should be touching each other.

Now you're ready to step up to home base to hit.

Next, rest the bat on your **right** shoulder, just to get comfortable.

If the coach says to go to the **left** side of home base, you go to the **left** just the way you are standing behind home base looking into the field. If you are **right-handed,** you go to the **left** side of home plate.

If you are **left-handed**, wrap the fingers of your **right** hand around the handle of the bat. Then, wrap the fingers of your **left** hand around the handle just above your right hand. Next, rest the bat on your **left** shoulder.

If the coach says to go to the **right** side of home base, you go to the **right.** If you're **left-handed,** you go to the **right** side of home plate.

I know it's a little hard to remember, but the more you bat, the more you'll begin to understand it.

There are many ways of hitting the ball. But most players usually begin to learn to hit by following these simple suggestions:

1 Stand several inches away from home plate so that when you stretch out your arms the **meat** of the bat (that's the big part) will be even with the ball on the Tee.

2 Spread your feet so that they are about the same distance apart as the distance between your shoulders. This is a little hard to see in your mind, so look closely at this photograph. Some batters feel more comfortable having their left foot a little ahead of the rest of their body.

3 Getting used to standing with a bat in your hands is not easy. When it comes to hitting, just as with almost everything else in Tee Ball, you should listen closely to what your coach has to say.

4 Next, lift the bat off your shoulder.

5

Tuck your chin into your shoulder. This helps you to keep your head from moving and helps you focus on watching the ball.

6

Move your elbows away from your body.

7

Bend your knees just a little. Getting into this stance may be hard to understand and could feel a little uncomfortable, so look closely at this photograph.

8

You are almost ready to swing the bat. But first, raise your back elbow, just a little. This will give you more power when you hit the ball.

9 Move the bat toward the ball, stretching your arms as you start to swing. You might want to do this several times slowly to practice what you're doing and to see how it feels.

10 At **the same time** that you swing, turn your shoulders and your hips toward the pitcher's mound.

11 While you are swinging the bat and turning your body, you should keep looking at the ball on the tee. Hitting the ball sounds very complicated, but it's really not as hard as it sounds. Look closely at the photos of the hitters. The more you practice, the easier it will become.

12 Once you have hit the ball, drop the bat on the ground and run toward first base. NEVER throw the bat. If you throw the bat, you may injure someone. NEVER throw the bat!

Congratulations! You have just hit the ball!

The **fielders** are the players who stand in the **field**, each at a different **position**.

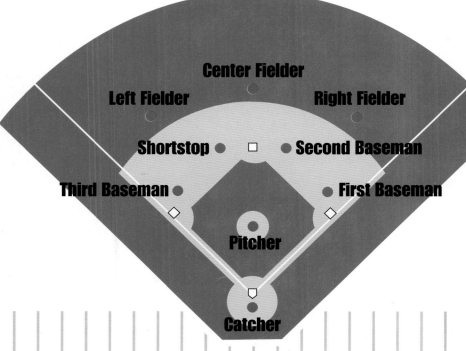

Center Fielder

Left Fielder

Right Fielder

Shortstop   Second Baseman

Third Baseman   First Baseman

Pitcher

Catcher

Here is a diagram of Tee Ball fielders.

13

The **First Baseman** stands near first base and catches the ball if the batter hits the ball near first base. He also stands with one foot on first base and catches the ball if another fielder throws it to first base.

The **Second Baseman** stands between first and second base, nearer to second base. He picks up the ball if the batter hits the ball near second base. He also stands on second base to catch the ball if another fielder throws the ball to him.

The **Shortstop** stands almost in the middle between second base and third base, sometimes a little nearer to second base. The shortstop catches the ball if the batter hits the ball in his area. Sometimes he stands on second base to catch the ball if another fielder throws him the ball.

The **Third Baseman** stands near third base and catches the ball if the batter hits the ball near third base. He also stands with one foot on third base and catches the ball if another fielder throws it to third base.

The **Left Fielder** stands in the **outfield**, usually about twenty or thirty feet behind the shortstop. This position is called **left field**, because if you stood on home plate, the left fielder would be on your left.

The **Center Fielder** stands about twenty or thirty feet behind second base. This position is in the **center** of the outfield.

The **Right Fielder** stands about twenty or thirty feet behind the first and second basemen, usually a little closer to the first baseman. This position is called **right field**, because if you stood on home plate, the right fielder would be on your right.

The left fielder, center fielder, and right fielder play in the **outfield**. It is called the outfield because it is "out" beyond the **infield**.

Usually in Tee Ball, the pitcher doesn't throw the ball because the ball is sitting on the tee. But you still need a pitcher to catch the ball if the batter hits it near the pitcher's mound.

In baseball the **Pitcher** stands on the **pitcher's mound** and throws the ball to the batter. Sometimes in Tee Ball, a coach will throw the ball to some of the hitters.

The **Catcher** crouches behind home plate and catches the ball thrown by the pitcher. The catcher also catches the ball if another fielder throws the ball to him. In baseball the catcher wears a mask, chest protector, and shin guards to be protected from the ball, which a pitcher throws hard. Many Tee Ball teams do not have a catcher because the ball is being hit off a tee.

The fielders wear **gloves** that they use to catch the ball.

Picking out a good baseball glove is an important part of learning how to catch the ball. Your hands right now are small, so you want to buy a glove that isn't too big for your hand. But remember, your hands are going to grow, and grow quickly, too. You probably won't want to buy a very expensive glove, because in a year or two, your hands may already be too big to use the glove you bought this year!

Once you have a glove, put your name on it right away. Then you will be able to find it easily if you toss it someplace with other gloves or if someone picks up your glove by mistake.

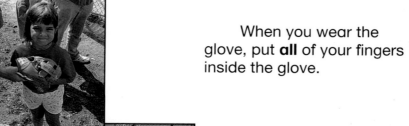

When you wear the glove, put **all** of your fingers inside the glove.

Put your name in your hat, too.

Catching the ball in the air is not as easy as it looks. It takes a lot of practice—**a lot** of practice.

So don't be discouraged if you can't catch the ball right away.

Catching the ball begins by watching the ball from the time it leaves another player's hand or from the time that it is hit **all the way** into your glove.

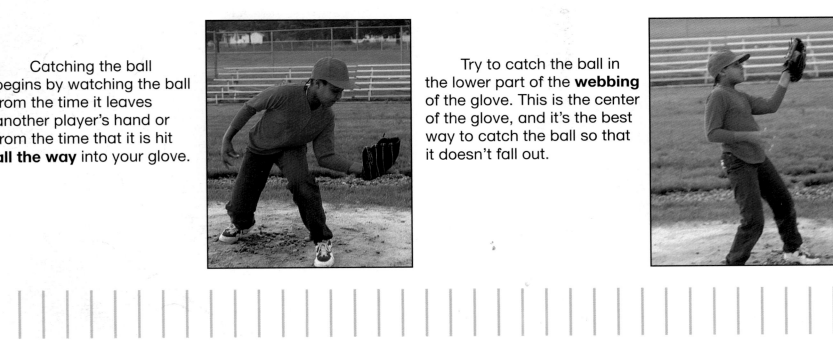

Try to catch the ball in the lower part of the **webbing** of the glove. This is the center of the glove, and it's the best way to catch the ball so that it doesn't fall out.

When you see and feel the ball in the glove, quickly close the glove shut on the ball and cover up the glove with your other hand. Covering up the ball in the glove with your other hand helps you hold on to the ball, and it also helps you get ready to take the ball out of the glove to throw it.

There are a couple of tips that players use that will help you catch the ball. First, if the ball is coming at you and the ball is **below your waist**, turn the glove so that the fingers of the glove are pointed toward the ground.

If the ball is coming at you and it is **above your waist**, turn the fingers of the glove toward the sky.

One of the hardest balls to catch is the one that comes right at you and is between your waist and your head! Sometimes you will turn the glove down. Sometimes you will turn it up. Sometimes you won't know what to do until the very last second!

To get used to catching the ball, stand about ten or fifteen feet away from another player, your parent, or a coach, and have them lightly toss the ball to you.

The **pop-up** or **fly ball** is also hard to catch. This happens when the ball is hit or thrown high in the air and it is coming down over your head toward you. First, turn the glove with your fingers toward the sky, and like all the other catches you've made, watch the ball all the way into your glove.

When the ball is hit on the ground, it's called a **grounder**. Grounders can be hard to catch, because the ball is bouncing on the ground, and you can't be sure what the ball is going to do.

To keep the ball from going past you, **get in front** of it.

This means that you have to move your feet quickly so that you are in front of the ball.

To catch the ball, turn the glove so that the fingers are pointed down. Bend your knees, so that you are almost squatting in front of the ball. Some players even get on one knee.

Watch the ball **all the way** into your glove. Close the glove, cover it with your other hand, and get ready to throw the ball.

To learn to throw the ball, first get used to how the ball feels. Toss the ball a few inches up in the air and catch it. Repeat this a few times, and you'll start to get an idea of how the ball feels and what way you like to hold the ball.

Grip the ball in your hand so that your fingers wrap around as much of the ball as possible. Your fingers will be very important in throwing the ball. In fact, you actually use your fingers a lot more than you use your hand when you throw the ball.

There are three things that a person throwing a ball tries to do: throw fast, throw far, and throw straight. Of the three, throwing **straight** is the most important. It doesn't matter how far or fast you throw if you can't throw the ball to the right person.

Here are a few tips to help you throw straight.

1

First, make sure that the teammate you're throwing to is looking at you and is ready to catch the ball.

2

Stand with your feet a little apart. Put your left foot slightly ahead of your right foot. (Left-handed throwers, put your right foot a little ahead of your left foot.) Then turn your hips and upper body a bit so that your right shoulder is behind your left shoulder. (Left-handers, turn your left shoulder.)

3

Next, pull your right arm back so that your hand passes by your right ear, almost as if you were getting ready to shoot an arrow. (Left-handers, pull your left arm back past your left ear.)

4

Bend your wrist slightly downward.

In one smooth motion...

6

Push your arm out in front of you as far as it can go and roll your hand forward.

5

Quickly bring the ball past your ear again.

7

Step forward with your left foot in the direction of your teammate.

8 Twist your shoulders and hip forward, and release the ball just as you finish stretching out your arm.

9 At the end of throwing the ball, your fingers should be pointing directly at the person you wanted to throw to.

This sounds a lot harder than it really is.

Throwing is a lot like hitting. The more you do it, the easier it will be.

The first rule of Tee Ball is to try to hit the ball and run to first base. After that, Tee Ball rules get harder to understand. You don't need to know all of these rules to have a good time playing Tee Ball, but here are a few more.

Once you are safely on a base, you are called the **runner**.

The **runner** wants to run from first base to second to third and to home base to score a run.

So if you were the runner on first base, you would want to run to second base. You would wait until the next batter hit the ball, then run as fast as you could to second base.

When the next batter hit the ball, you would run to third base.

And when the next batter hit the ball, you would run to home plate.

The fielders want to stop the runner by getting the runner or the batter out.

Making an Out

When you are first learning how to play Tee Ball, making an out is not important. But if you continue to play Tee Ball and if you want to play baseball, you will need to know about making an out. Being out means that you cannot go to the next base.

If you are called out, you go to the bench to sit with your teammates and wait until you get another chance to hit the ball.

There are many ways to make an out. Here are three.

Fly Out

If you hit the ball into the air, one of the fielders will try to catch the ball in the air. If the fielder catches the ball **before** it hits the ground, then you are **out**. You have **flied out**.

Ground Out

If you hit the ball on the ground, one of the fielders may pick up the ball and throw it to the first baseman. If the first baseman catches the ball and touches first base **before** you get to first base, then you are also **out**.

Tag Out

The fielder can also catch the ball and **tag** a base runner with the ball. Then the base runner would be **tagged out**.

But whether you get a hit, score a run, or make an out, remember, the purpose of playing Tee Ball . . .

... is to have FUN!

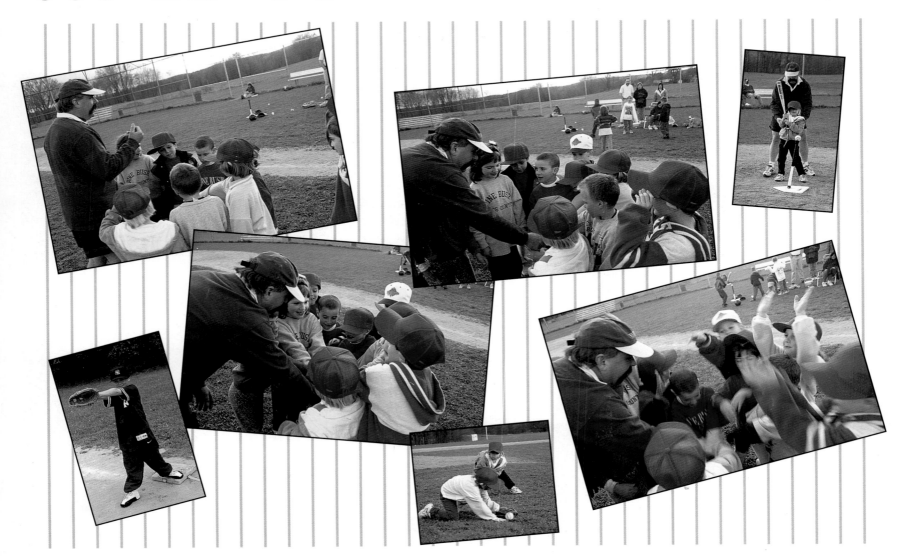

THANKS TO

Brittany Albronda
William Albronda
William Albronda, Jr.
Jesse Buxton
Josiah Buxton
Jon J. Buxton
Julia Cheripko
Mark Huston Dodson
Nicholas Drewchin
Ayden Fiorelli
Andy Gutelle
Jessica Henderson
Tina Hoehn-Figura
Ryan Kimball
Bennie Landman

Scott Leet
John Lenihan
Becky Loring
Samuel Miller
Taylor Murray
Jonathan Nardi
Shannon Nolan
Annie O'Brien
Eric Orr
Thomas Papesca
Emma Pecoraro
Marie Perry
Sam Pursch
Tony Randall
Matt Savastano

Teena Schueler
Bethany Stachowiak
Rose Stachowiak
Chris Stein
Mark Talmadge
Mike Tanagretta
Paul Terwilleger
Bill Voegelin
Shanice Wadell
Rich Wallace
Jeremy Watson
Arlene Williamson
Jim Williamson
Tyler Williamson
Samantha Zimmer

INDEX